# The Landscape of Ke

C000246127

AMBASSADOR |

SALMON

Published by J Salmon Limited
100 London Road, Sevenoaks, Kent TN13 1BB

First edition 2000

Designed by the Salmon Studio

Copyright © 2000 J Salmon Limited

ISBN 1 898435 80 4

All rights reserved. No part of this publication may be reproduced, stored in a retrieval system, or transmitted, in any form or by any means, electronic, mechanical, photocopying, recording or otherwise, nor may any of the illustrations be framed, mounted or converted in any manner for resale, without the prior permission of the copyright holder.

Neither this book nor any part or any of the photographs or reproductions contained in it shall be sold or disposed of otherwise than as a complete book and any unauthorised sale of such part, illustration, photograph or reproduction shall be deemed to be a breach of the Publisher's Copyright.

Printed in England by
J Salmon Limited, Tubs Hill Works, Sevenoaks, Kent.

Front cover: Oast houses near Penshurst
Back cover: Scotney Castle
Title page: Rolvenden Mill

Time Ball Tower, Deal

# CONTENTS

CANTERBURY AND THE NORTH DOWNS 6

THE WEALD OF KENT 20

ROMNEY MARSH AND THE CINQUE PORTS 28

WEST KENT 38

ROCHESTER AND THE NORTH KENT COAST 50

INDEX 60

# Introduction

The county of Kent has been given many epithets - "The Garden of England", "The Gateway of England", "The Cradle of English Christianity". Its historical associations go back into mists of time and the Cantii, who gave their tribal name to the shire and to Canterbury, were in possession when Caesar landed in 55BC. Other early visitors included the Jutish kings Hengist and Horsa, and St. Augustine in 597; Kent inspired Geoffrey Chaucer in the fourteenth century and Charles Dickens in the nineteenth.

The scenery of Kent is as varied as it is beautiful. From west to east across the middle of the county runs the broad chalk ridge of the North Downs, rising over 800 feet at its highest point. An isolated outcrop forms the Isle of Thanet, with low chalk cliffs, but the famous "White Cliffs of England" lie at the eastern end of the Downs, on either side of Dover Harbour. South of the Downs comes the Weald. From the sixteenth century to the eighteenth, the Kent and Sussex Weald was the "Black Country" of England, the centre of the iron-smelting trade. Today, whilst still retaining extensive areas of oak woodland, it is a pastoral landscape dotted with red-tiled villages and oasthouses set amidst the orchards and hopgardens.

It is only natural that a county so richly endowed with attractive scenery, and such a variety of building materials, should contain a great number of fine buildings of all periods. Quite apart from such obvious examples as Canterbury and Rochester cathedrals and Dover and Rochester castles, Kent displays an unrivalled collection of beautiful country-houses. Like the parish churches, these large houses and castles of the medieval, Tudor and Elizabethan periods were built mainly of stone. Among these are Hever Castle, Ightham Mote, Leeds Castle and Penshurst Place, perhaps the most perfect mediaeval house in England. Knole near Sevenoaks, also built of stone, is crammed with fine craftsmanship, furniture and pictures. Contemporary to these large mansions, beautiful half-timbered yeomen's houses were being constructed of oak from the Wealden forests.

As for beautiful villages and small towns, they are numerous and include delightful Chiddingstone, Penshurst, Chilham, Goudhurst, Tenterden and Sandwich, as well as many more less frequented by the visitor.

◁ Winter at Penshurst

# CANTERBURY AND THE NORTH DOWNS

## Canterbury

With its wealth of fine old buildings, is still partly enclosed by medieval walls. The narrow lanes of the old town can best be seen around Christchurch Gate which leads into the cathedral precincts. The glory of the city is, without doubt, its cathedral. Founded by St. Augustine in 602, the present structure was begun in 1070 but many additions were made over the next 500 years, culminating in the splendid central Bell Harry Tower. Over the centuries large numbers of pilgrims have been drawn here, a fact which is immortalised in Chaucer's famous *Canterbury Tales*.

◁ Christchurch Gate, Canterbury
The east end, Canterbury Cathedral ▷

## Chillenden

Lying between Canterbury and the sea, Chillenden is an ancient village associated with Thomas Chillenden, the 14th century prior under whose direction the nave of Canterbury Cathedral was rebuilt. The Griffin's Head Inn dates from his time and there is also a tiny flint-built church. Just north of the church stands an attractive open-trestle post mill. It was built in 1868 to replace an earlier structure which stood on the same site in the 17th century.

## Fordwich

Two miles north-east of Canterbury, Fordwich on the River Stour was a thriving port in medieval times and is still centred around the old quay where ships once unloaded wine and other goods from the continent. Among the remarkable old buildings grouped around the 18th century hump-backed bridge are ancient cottages, inns and the impressive Church of St. Mary the Virgin. It retains some Saxon work but dates mainly from the 13th century and includes a tomb in which it is said that St. Augustine once lay.

◁ Chillenden Mill
Cottages at Fordwich ▷

## Chilham

Standing astride the old Pilgrims' Way which leads to Becket's shrine at Canterbury, Chilham has many fine half-timbered houses, shops and inns which date from the late Middle Ages. Among its historic buildings are the remains of an archbishop's palace where Thomas Cranmer lived and Henry VIII once stayed. In the heart of the village is the 15th century White Horse. Near it, at one corner of the attractive square, stands St. Mary's Church with its 15th century flint and stone tower.

## Patrixbourne

Situated just outside Canterbury in the Nailbourne Valley, Patrixborne is another delightful village of half-timbered houses. The church was built around 1170 and has some outstanding carving, notably on the main door where grotesque heads, animals and leaves surround the figure of Christ among the angels. There is also some remarkable stained glass which dates from the 16th and 17th centuries.

◁ The Square, Chilham
St. Mary's Church, Patrixbourne ▷

## Willesborough

One of several old villages which surround
Ashford, Willesborough has a church
with an intriguing 'candle-snuffer' spire.
Willesborough Mill is a fine white-painted
smock mill which dates from 1869 when it
was built to replace an earlier mill which had
fallen into disrepair on the same site. Now
restored, it is a well-known landmark on the
route across Kent to the continent.

## Godmersham

A village on the River Stour, Godmersham
is closely associated with Jane Austen. Her
brother Edward changed his surname to
Knight in order to inherit the manor of
Godmersham in the 1790s and the novelist
herself often stayed at Godmersham Park.
She probably drew on her memories of this
fine Georgian brick mansion when she
wrote *Mansfield Park*. There is a memorial
to Edward Knight on the north wall of the
church which retains some 11th century
Norman work and has a late Saxon tower.
An early medieval carving in the church is
believed to represent Thomas Becket, seated
below his cathedral.

◁ Willesborough Mill
St. Lawrence's Church, Godmersham ▷

## Charing

Set beneath the slopes of the downs, Charing is noteworthy for the remains of the Archbishop's Palace which stands close by the church. It was built for a 14th century Archbishop of Canterbury and at a later date Henry VIII stayed here on his way to France. The gate-house still stands and within the ruins is a farmhouse added in Tudor times. The church was badly damaged by fire in 1590 and the magnificent tower dates from the rebuilding which took place at this time.

## Great Chart

Once a much larger place than it is today, Great Chart is closely associated with Godinton House, the nearby home of the Toke family who were lords of the manor and local landowners for more than 500 years. The church at Great Chart contains many monuments and brasses of the Toke family and in the churchyard there is a tiny timber and stone hall known as the Pest House. Dating from the 15th century, it was apparently used to isolate plague victims. A number of attractive tile-hung, gabled cottages line the main street in the village.

◁ The Archbishop's Palace, Charing
The Pest House, Great Chart ▷

## Leeds Castle

Standing in idyllic surroundings, its stone walls rising directly from the lake, Leeds Castle was originally constructed by a Norman baron in the 12th century and the castle is rich in historic associations. In 1278 it passed into the ownership of the royal family and Edward I spent much time here with his queen, Eleanor of Castile. Later it became the home of Henry VIII's first wife, Catherine of Aragon. The castle now houses a treasure store of art and antiques while in the grounds there is a delightful garden of old-fashioned flowers and a vineyard which was first recorded in the Domesday Book.

## Otham

Clinging to the hillside in an area where quarrying for ragstone was carried on over many centuries is the village of Otham. It boasts a number of fine half-timbered buildings, many of which resulted from the prosperity which the quarrying brought with it. Among these is Stoneacre, an outstanding yeoman's house built around 1480 and now owned by the National Trust. It has a fine Hall and the garden, extending over some fourteen acres, has recently been restored to its former glory.

◁ Leeds Castle
Stoneacre, Otham ▷

**Heaverham**

One of a number of attractive villages in this area, Heaverham stands on the route of the Pilgrim's Way, the path used for centuries by pilgrims travelling to Canterbury. A familiar sight across the county, the oast house with its conical roof and white cap was originally a kiln for drying hops. Many have now been converted into homes and this attractive group near Heaverham typifies the quiet rural charm of the area.

**Eynsford**

With its timbered houses and narrow stone bridge beside a ford, Eynsford is a delightful village which features frequently in the work of artists and photographers. It is also an ancient village, through which the Romans must have travelled on their way to build the villa at nearby Lullingstone. There are several old cottages of considerable interest in Eynsford, notably in the lane which leads to the ford. Close by the River Darenth are the remains of a small Norman castle, built in about 1100. A good deal of the curtain wall still stands, reaching a height of 30 feet in places. Also near the river is the church which dates from Norman times and has a tower surmounted by a slim, wood-shingled spire.

◁ Cottages and oast houses, Heaverham
River Darenth, Eynsford ▷

# THE WEALD OF KENT

## Smallhythe

Lying on the Rother Levels between Tenterden and the Isle of Oxney, Smallhythe was a prosperous port and ship-building centre in the Middle Ages when the River Rother was wider and deeper. In 1538 Henry VIII came here to inspect a warship which was under construction. Smallhythe Place is an impressive half-timbered Kentish yeoman's house which was originally built in about 1480 for the harbourmaster. From 1899 to 1928 the famous actress Ellen Terry lived here and the house contains many mementoes of her life.

## Tenterden

A typical Wealden town, Tenterden was an important wool-trading centre in the 15th century and the main street is one of the most attractive in the south of England. Bordered by trees and grass verges, it contains a number of bow-fronted Georgian shops with fine timber-clad frontages. Also owing its splendid size to the prosperity which came from wool, is the church, with its rare dedication to St. Mildred. The tall, pinnacled West Tower was built in 1461 with the support of Flemish weavers who lived in the town.

◁ Smallhythe Place
High Street, Tenterden ▷

## Biddenden

Picturesque Biddenden is one of the prettiest of Wealden villages. Many of its timbered weavers' cottages date from the 15th century and its footpaths are paved with rough hewn blocks of stone. A sign on the village green commemorates Biddenden's most famous residents, Siamese twins known as the 'Maids of Biddenden.' Believed to have been born around 1100, they lived, joined at hip and shoulder, to the age of thirty-four.

## Headcorn

Although it is a busy little town today, Headcorn still possesses some attractive old houses from past centuries. Many of them were built by merchants in the cloth trade from which much Wealden prosperity came. A row of cottages leads from the church to Headcorn Manor. It was built in 1516 as the parsonage and the central hall is lit by an outstanding oriel window.

◁ The Green, Biddenden
The Old Parsonage, Headcorn ▷

## Sissinghurst Castle

Noted for it's beautiful gardens
which were created in the
1930s by Vita Sackville-West
and her husband, Harold
Nicholson, Sissinghurst Castle
stands in the midst of the
Weald. They consist of a
number of themed gardens,
including a White Garden
and a Cottage Garden, which
are linked by narrow paths
between hedges and walls.
Filled with colour throughout
the year, the Cottage Garden is
planted predominantly in shades
of orange and yellow. The
library and study where the
writer and poet worked can
also be seen.

## Cranbrook

The centre of the clothmaking
industry in Kent in medieval
times Cranbrook benefited
from the plentiful supply of
trees to provide timber for the
construction of fulling mills
and ample streams to drive
the mills. The magnificent
parish church dates from this
period and there are many
picturesque old buildings
lining Cranbrook's streets.
The Union Mill, said to be
the finest smock mill in the
country, stands high above
the eastern end of the town.

◁ Sissinghurst Castle
Union Mill, Cranbrook ▷

## Scotney Castle

A mile to the south of
Lamberhurst, Scotney Castle
is a delightful combination of
ancient ruins, formal flower
beds, wooded slopes and a
lake where water lilies bloom.
It was a 19th century owner
of the castle, Edward Hussey,
who had the vision to leave
the most visually pleasing
parts of the original medieval
and Tudor building standing
when he built a new house
on the slopes above the lake.
Scotney is particularly known
for the profusion of flowering
shrubs, including rhododendrons,
azaleas and wistaria, which
surround the ruins of the
14th century moated castle.

## Goudhurst

Occupying a commanding
position on top of a hill which
offers magnificent views of the
Wealden orchards, oasts and
hop-gardens which are spread
out below is the pretty village
of Goudhurst. From the tower
of St. Mary's Church, which
dates from the 13th and 14th
centuries, the panorama
extends on a clear day from
Rochester in the north to
Hastings on the south coast.
The village has an abundance
of the distinctive tile-hung,
white weather-boarded houses
which are so typical of the
area. Although it is a tranquil
spot today, Goudhurst was
frequented by smugglers in the
18th century at which time a
tunnel connected the Star and
Eagle Hotel to the church.

◁ Scotney Castle
Cottages and church, Goudhurst ▷

# ROMNEY MARSH AND THE CINQUE PORTS

## Fairfield Church

Romney Marsh is an area of isolated hamlets and communities, most of them served by their own churches. The Romney Marsh Historic Churches Trust was formed twenty years ago to work for the preservation of the fourteen medieval churches which survive. The Church of St. Thomas à Becket at Fairfield is surrounded by marshland which is subject to flooding so that, until the causeway was built, church-goers often had to arrive by boat. A church has stood here since Norman times but brick cladding was added in the early 1900s to protect the wooden structure.

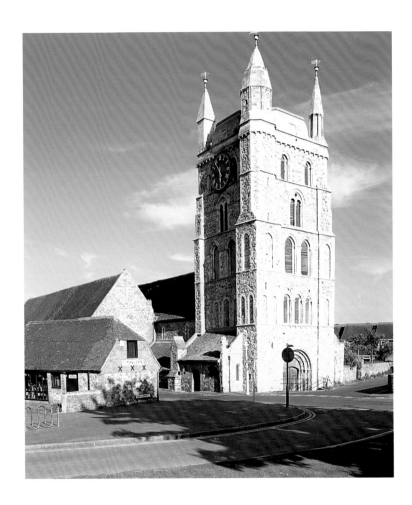

## New Romney

The main town on Romney Marsh, New Romney once boasted no fewer than four churches. The town owed much of its prosperity to the sea and the only one of these churches which survives is dedicated to St. Nicholas, patron saint of sailors. A magnificent combination of Norman and Early English architecture, the church has a fine Norman west door and a massive west tower which reaches a height of 100 feet. Once there was also a spire, which served as a land-mark for shipping, but this was demolished in the 1700s.

◁ St. Thomas à Becket's Church, Fairfield
St. Nicholas's Church, New Romney ▷

## Hythe

Lying at the eastern end of Dymchurch Bay, Hythe was one of the original Cinque Ports. Steps lead down from the promenade on to the sand and shingle beach where the fishermen's boats are often drawn up well clear of the sea. The town centre, now some half a mile inland, has a quiet charm with handsome mainly 18th century houses lining the hilly streets.

## Dungeness

Situated on a shingle promontory at the edge of Romney Marsh, Dungeness is famous for its lighthouses, its power station and its excellent fishing. It is also an important bird reserve and observatory. There has been a lighthouse on the promontory since 1615 and, in addition to the graceful modern structure, the remains of two earlier lighthouses can still be seen. As Dungeness has no harbour, fishermen draw their boats high up on the beach when they are not at sea.

◁ Fishing boats on Dungeness beach
Fishermen's Beach, Hythe ▷

**Dover**

The chief of the ancient Cinque Ports, Dover today is known as a terminus for cross-Channel ferries. The town is popular with holiday-makers and the vast outer harbour is well used both by dinghies and windsurfers. Built on a site which has been fortified since pre-historic times, Dover Castle has a rich and eventful history. Strategically positioned on a high hill above the famous White Cliffs, this impressive fortress with its 95 feet high keep dominates both the town and the harbour.

**Folkestone**

Until the 19th century, Folkestone was scarcely more than a cluster of fishermen's cottages around the harbour but it has now become a modern resort and channel port with many attractions for visitors. The narrow High Street, lined with ancient houses, runs steeply down to the harbour which pleasure boats now share with the fishing boats. Known for its fine cliff walks and gardens, including the famous Leas Gardens, Folkestone has an excellent sandy beach to the east of the harbour.

◁ The Harbour, Folkestone
    Dover Castle ▷

**St. Margaret's Bay**

A sheltered cove of shingle
and rocks St. Margaret's Bay
is situated not far from the
historic town of Deal. It enjoys
a very mild climate and, as
the nearest point to France,
has been the starting place for
many cross-Channel swimmers.
A steep, narrow road zig-zags
up the cliffs to the village of
St. Margaret's at Cliffe which
centres around its little Norman
church where smugglers once
stored their equipment.

**Walmer Castle**

Built by Henry VIII as part of
his coastal defences Walmer
castle is now the official
residence of the Lord Warden
of the Cinque Ports. It contains
many relics of former holders
of this office including the
Duke of Wellington who died
here in 1852. The delightful
castle gardens were originally
laid out in the 18th century under
the direction of Lady Hester
Stanhope and include colourful
herbaceous borders.

◁ St. Margaret's Bay
Walmer Castle ▷

## Sandwich

The northernmost of the original Cinque Ports, in the Middle Ages Sandwich was a bustling port. Now it lies almost two miles inland although the winding River Stour is still navigable to the open sea. A fascinating old town of twisting streets and medieval churches, Sandwich was at one time an important gateway to England and, as such, was heavily fortified. The Barbican Gate, constructed in 1539, guarded the northern approach to the town and now overlooks a narrow swing bridge across the Stour.

## Richborough Castle

An important fortress in Roman times when the Isle of Thanet was truly an island, Richborough Castle is separated from the mainland by the River Wantsum. It guarded the entrance to the river and the port of Rutupiae which was the chief point of entry for the Roman legions. The imposing walls of the castle are among the best preserved Roman walls in England, being twelve feet thick and up to twenty-four feet high in places. A museum near the entrance contains some of the fascinating objects found during excavations on the site.

◁ The Barbican, Sandwich
Richborough Castle ▷

# WEST KENT

## Royal Tunbridge Wells

One of the most elegant towns in the country, Royal Tunbridge Wells rivalled Bath as a spa town in Regency times. It is still possible to sample the waters of the Chalybeate Spring on which the town's reputation was founded. Discovered in 1606, it is located in the Pantiles, an attractive 18th century parade, lined with Italianate columns. Among the royal visitors to the town have been Queen Henrietta Maria, wife of Charles I, and Queen Anne but it was Edward VII who added 'Royal' to the town's name in 1909.

## Groombridge

The village of Groombridge has many fine old houses and cottages but it is renowned for "The Walks". This charming row of brick, tiled and weather-boarded cottages stands near the Crown Inn overlooking the little triangular green. Close by is Groombridge Place which dates from the late 17th century and has been attributed to Christopher Wren. Set in an extensive park, the mansion is surrounded by superb gardens which include herbaceous borders, topiary, fountains and a woodland area with a string of pools.

◁ The Pantiles, Royal Tunbridge Wells
The Walks, Groombridge ▷

## Penshurst

Dominated by Penshurst Place where Sir Philip Sidney was born in 1554 and his descendants still live, Penshurst stands in the valley of the River Medway. Among many picturesque corners in the village is Leicester Square which contains a number of attractive timbered cottages and an ancient lychgate leading into the churchyard. The church, which is partly 13th century, contains impressive memorials to the Sidney family.

## Chiddingstone

Another unspoilt Wealden village, Chiddingstone has several handsome 16th and 17th century houses which are now preserved for the future by the National Trust. Opposite the large sandstone church is a striking row of timber-framed houses, built when the iron industry brought wealth to this essentially rural area. Behind the street is the Chiding Stone, a large sandstone outcrop which is said by some to be the origin of the village name. Nearby stands the splendid 18th century mansion known as Chiddingstone Castle.

◁ Leicester Square, Penshurst
Cottages and church, Chiddingstone ▷

## Knole

One of the most impressive country houses in all England, Knole is surrounded by a large deer park, stands on the outskirts of Sevenoaks. Dating from 1456, it includes a splendid Tudor hall and notable state rooms which contain fine portraits, silver, tapestries and 17th century English furniture. The house is said to have 7 courtyards, 52 staircases and 365 rooms, corresponding with the days and weeks of the year. The gardens, in both formal and natural styles, remain little changed since the 17th century.

## Ightham Mote

Set in a peaceful and secluded valley near the village of Ivy Hatch, Ightham Mote is one of the loveliest and most important moated houses in the country. It probably takes its name not from its moat, but because it stands where the moot, or Saxon council, used to meet. The earliest parts of the mansion, including the Great Hall and the Old Chapel and crypt, date from 1340 while the famous panelled Tudor Chapel was added in 1520. The National Trust now owns Ightham Mote and has mounted a fascinating exhibition showing conservation work in action.

◁ The West Front, Knole
Ightham Mote ▷

## Hever Castle

Originally a 13th century fortified manor house, Hever Castle later became the home of Anne Boleyn, second wife of Henry VIII and mother of Queen Elizabeth I. It was restored in the early 1900s by William Waldorf Astor who made many alterations to the interior and added a village of Tudor-style cottages outside the moat. He also created the formal Italian garden as a setting for the classical sculptures he brought back from Italy. The magnificent grounds also include a rose garden, herb garden, maze and lake.

## Chartwell

Near Westerham, Chartwell was the family home of Sir Winston Churchill from 1924 until his death. It is set amongst fine gardens and there are spectacular views across the Weald of Kent from the grounds which include terraced gardens, a lake with black swans and a fish pond. The rooms are kept as they were in Churchill's time and contain many family possessions and items dating from his fifty years as a parliamentarian and statesman.

◁ Hever Castle
Chartwell ▷

## Tonbridge

An ancient market town Tonbridge stands on the River Medway at the upper limit of navigation and has, for this reason, been strategically important from the earliest times. The Saxons had a fortress here and it was also an important Norman stronghold. The ruins of the fine Norman castle stand high above the river. The castle was slighted by Parliamentarian forces during the Civil War but the magnificent 13th century gatehouse still stands up to three storeys high.

## Offham

Situated not far from West Malling, Offham is an attractive village with a number of dignified old houses, some of them timber-framed. The village has grown up around a small triangular green which boasts a rare, if not unique, survival – an ancient quintain. Similar equipment was used by knights for jousting practice but this example was probably used by the young men of the village who would approach on horseback to hit the swinging board and ride quickly away before the sandbag suspended at the other end swung round to unseat them.

◁ Tonbridge Castle
The Quintain, Offham ▷

## Sandling

Near Maidstone, Sandling is the location of The Museum of Kent Life which reflects the changes which have come about during the last century in the Garden of England. Here can be seen a working oast house, alongside displays of rural crafts and agricultural equipment as well as herb and kitchen gardens and orchards growing traditional Kentish varieties of fruit.

## Maidstone

Standing astride the River Medway in the heart of rich farmland, Maidstone has been a market centre since the Middle Ages. The River Medway was one of the main trade routes across the county but is now used largely for recreation. Among the historic buildings in the town is the Archbishop's Palace, which dates mainly from the Elizabethan era. For more than 300 years it was a residence of the Archbishop of Canterbury and now houses a local Heritage Centre.

◁ Oast houses at Sandling
Archbishop's Palace, Maidstone ▷

# ROCHESTER AND THE NORTH KENT COAST

## Rochester

The city of Rochester has been inhabited since pre-Roman times and the castle, high above the River Medway, was built by William the Conqueror. The Keep stands 125 feet high and, together with its four corner turrets, is one of the best-preserved in England. Rochester Cathedral, the second oldest cathedral in England, stands opposite the castle. It was founded by St. Augustine in AD 604 but the present building, with its magnificent West Front, dates mainly from Norman times. College Gate, one of three surviving 15th century gateways in the city, leads into the cathedral precincts but many of the city's other ancient buildings are to be found in the High Street, including the Corn Exchange and Eastgate House which houses the Charles Dickens Centre. The city is closely associated with the author who lived at nearby Gad's Hill for the last twelve years of his life.

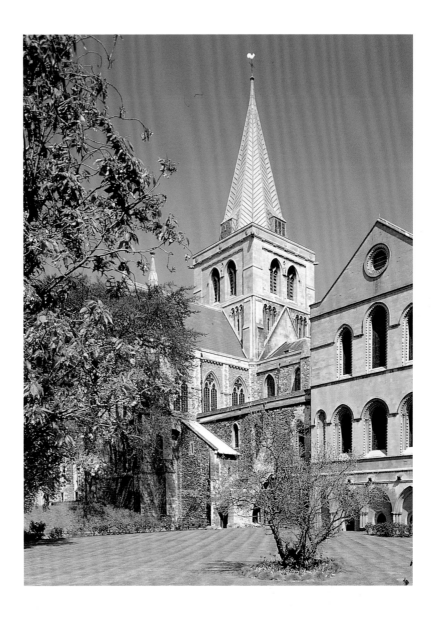

◁ Eastgate House, Rochester

Rochester Cathedral ▷

## Meopham

An ancient village which straggles for some two miles along the road, Meopham is flanked by wooded downland countryside. The village is associated with many famous cricketers, including W.G.Grace who once played cricket on Meopham Green. Still with its cricket pitch and pavilion, the little triangular green is overlooked by a fine, hexagonal smock mill. Built in 1801 this impressive five-storey mill ceased to work in 1929 but has since been restored and is now able to grind corn once again.

## Cobham

A downland village of exceptional interest, Cobham church houses a collection of memorial brasses which is among the most outstanding in the country. Set in a park to the east of the church is Cobham Hall, a fine Tudor mansion which was the home of the lords of the manor. Behind the church are the remains of New College, which dates from 1370 and was used as almshouses for much of that time. Opposite the churchyard stands a fine timbered inn, The Leather Bottle, which was mentioned by Charles Dickens in his novel *Pickwick Papers*.

◁ Meopham Mill
The Leather Bottle, Cobham ▷

## Faversham

Situated on a creek of the River Swale, Faversham was once a flourishing port and the bustling quayside is still used by yachts and other small boats. The town has a wealth of fine Tudor, Stuart and Georgian buildings. The impressive timber-framed Arden's House once served as the gatehouse to a Benedictine Abbey, founded in 1147. It is named after Thomas Arden, a wealthy merchant and town mayor, who acquired the house in the 16th century. The priory church of Davington Priory, founded six years after the abbey, is now used as Davington Parish Church.

## Whitstable

Renowned since Roman times for its oysters, Whitstable still retains many features of its seafaring past. Weather-boarded fishermen's cottages and old boat sheds stand around the harbour which is still used by small coasters and oyster yawls. There is good bathing and fishing from the shingle beach and at low tide boats are left on the mud flats by the receding tide. Whitstable Castle, originally known as Tankerton Tower, is a fine castellated mansion with an octagonal tower which probably dates from the 15th century.

◁ Davington Priory, Faversham
Whitstable Harbour ▷

## Reculver

The main landmark along the ten mile stretch of coast between Herne Bay and Margate are the twin towers of St. Mary's Church, Reculver. The church was undermined by the sea and demolished during the 19th century but the towers, which date from the 12th century, were restored without their original spires by Trinity House, as an aid to Thames estuary shipping. There are clifftop paths which lead walkers over Beacon Hill towards Reculver.

## The North Foreland

Situated a short walk from Broadstairs along the top of the cliffs is the North Foreland. Here the lighthouse overlooks the busy shipping lanes at the entrance to the Thames estuary and warns shipping away from the twelve-mile-long sand bar known as the Goodwin Sands. A light has stood on this spot since at least 1634 and a candle-powered lighthouse may have existed here as early as 1505.

◁ St. Mary's Church, Reculver
North Foreland Lighthouse ▷

## Broadstairs

A favourite resort with visitors since Georgian times Broadstairs is known for its narrow twisting streets, attractive corners and numerous sheltered sandy bays. The town is closely associated with Charles Dickens who stayed at Bleak House when he was writing David Copperfield. The castellated, fort-like building overlooks a small but busy harbour which is protected by a short curving pier.

## Ramsgate

Probably best known today as a seaside resort with sandy, south-facing beaches Ramsgate has been a Channel port since Roman times and the harbour around which the town is built is one of the busiest on the south coast. As well as a modern yacht marina, it has many points of historic interest which are displayed in the Maritime Museum and through the Historic Harbour Trail. An obelisk commemorates the landing here of George IV in 1822, since when it has been known as the "Royal Harbour".

◁ The harbour, Broadstairs
Maritime Museum, Ramsgate ▷

# Index

| | | | | |
|---|---|---|---|---|
| Broadstairs | 59 | Knole | 42 |
| Biddenden | 22 | Leeds Castle | 16 |
| Canterbury | 6 | Maidstone | 48 |
| Canterbury Cathedral | 7 | Meopham | 52 |
| Charing | 14 | New Romney | 29 |
| Chartwell | 45 | North Foreland Lighthouse | 57 |
| Chiddingstone | 41 | Ofham | 47 |
| Chilham | 10 | Otham | 17 |
| Chillenden Mill | 8 | Patrixbourne | 11 |
| Cobham | 52 | Penshurst | 41 |
| Cranbrook | 25 | Ramsgate | 59 |
| Dover | 33 | Reculver | 56 |
| Dungeness | 30 | Richborough Castle | 37 |
| Eynesford | 19 | Rochester | 51 |
| Fairfield | 29 | Rochester Cathedral | 51 |
| Faversham | 54 | Royal Tunbridge Wells | 39 |
| Folkestone | 33 | Sandling | 48 |
| Fordwich | 9 | Sandwich | 37 |
| Godmersham | 13 | Scotney Castle | 27 |
| Goudhurst | 27 | Sissinghurst Castle | 25 |
| Great Chart | 15 | Smallhythe | 20 |
| Groombridge | 39 | St. Margaret's Bay | 34 |
| Headcorn | 22 | Tenterden | 21 |
| Heaverham | 18 | Tonbridge Castle | 46 |
| Hever Castle | 45 | Walmer Castle | 34 |
| Hythe | 30 | Whitstable | 54 |
| Ightham Mote | 42 | Willesborough | 12 |